THE POWER

A

HEALTHY FINANCIAL MINDSET

Muhammad Patel

Table of Contents

INTRODUCTION

The Importance of Financial Health

Financial health is an essential component of overall well-being. Just as physical and mental health contribute to a fulfilling life, so does financial health. It encompasses more than just having money; it involves having the security and freedom to live life on your own terms, make choices that align with your values, and handle life's inevitable ups and downs with confidence. Achieving financial health means having a balanced approach to earning, saving, spending, and investing, allowing you to meet your current needs while preparing for the future.

When you are financially healthy, you experience less stress and anxiety about money, which can significantly improve your mental and physical health. You can plan for major life events, such as buying a home, starting a family, or retiring comfortably, without constant worry. Financial health also enables you to seize opportunities, whether they are personal or professional, and to support causes and people you care about.

Understanding Your Relationship with Money

Everyone has a unique relationship with money, shaped by personal experiences, upbringing, cultural influences, and societal norms. Understanding this relationship is crucial for developing a healthy financial mindset. Reflect on the messages about money you received growing up, the habits you've formed over the years, and how money influences your emotions and decisions. Are there patterns of fear, guilt, or shame associated with your financial behavior? Or perhaps a sense of empowerment and control?

This self-awareness is the first step in transforming your financial mindset. It helps you recognize destructive patterns and replace them with constructive habits. By understanding your relationship with money, you can shift from a mindset of scarcity and anxiety to one of abundance and purpose. This transformation is not about accumulating wealth for its own sake but about achieving a state where money serves you and enhances your life, rather than dictating it.

How to Use This Book

"Mindful Wealth: Cultivating a Healthy Financial Mindset" is designed to guide you through a comprehensive journey toward financial health. This book is structured to be both informative and practical, offering insights, strategies, and exercises to help you build a solid financial foundation and maintain a positive relationship with money.

Each chapter focuses on a different aspect of financial health, from foundational principles to specific strategies for budgeting, saving, and investing. You'll find practical tips, real-life examples, and actionable steps to implement immediately. Here's how to get the most out of this book:

1. **Read Sequentially or Selectively**: If you prefer a structured approach, read the chapters in order. Each chapter builds on the previous one, providing a cohesive path to financial well-being. Alternatively, you can jump to specific sections that address your immediate needs or interests.

2. **Engage with the Exercises**: Throughout the book, you'll find exercises and worksheets designed to help you apply the concepts to your own life. Take the time to complete these exercises, as they are crucial for translating knowledge into action.

3. **Reflect and Revisit**: Building a healthy financial mindset is an ongoing process. Reflect on your progress regularly and revisit chapters as needed. The financial landscape changes, and so do your personal circumstances. This book can be a continual resource as you navigate these changes.

4. **Utilize the Resources**: The appendices include a glossary, recommended readings, and additional resources. These can deepen your understanding and keep you informed about financial matters.

5. **Stay Committed**: Transformation takes time and effort. Stay committed to your financial journey, and remember that setbacks are a part of growth. Use this book as a steady guide to help you stay on track and motivated.

By the end of this book, you will have not only the knowledge but also the mindset and tools necessary to achieve and maintain financial health.

CHAPTER ONE

FOUNDATIONS OF FINANCIAL WELL-BEING

Defining Financial Health

Financial health is a multifaceted concept that goes beyond simply having a high income or substantial savings. It encompasses a holistic view of your financial situation, including your ability to manage daily finances, prepare for financial emergencies, and plan for future financial goals. Financial health can be defined through the following key dimensions:

1. **Cash Flow Management**: This involves your ability to manage your income and expenses effectively. Positive cash flow, where your income exceeds your expenses, is a fundamental aspect of financial health.
2. **Debt Management**: Healthy financial practices include managing debt wisely. This means maintaining manageable debt levels and having a clear strategy for repaying debts. It's important to differentiate between "good debt," which can provide long-term benefits (like a mortgage or student loans), and "bad debt" (like high-interest credit card debt).
3. **Savings and Investments**: Having sufficient savings for emergencies and investing for long-term goals, such as retirement, are crucial. Financial health means not only saving but also investing wisely to grow your wealth over time.

4. **Risk Management**: This includes having adequate insurance coverage to protect against unforeseen events, such as medical emergencies, natural disasters, or loss of income.
5. **Financial Literacy**: Understanding basic financial concepts and being able to make informed decisions is essential for maintaining financial health. This includes knowledge of budgeting, saving, investing, and understanding credit and loans.
6. **Future Planning**: This involves setting and working towards long-term financial goals, such as buying a home, funding children's education, or planning for retirement. It also includes estate planning and preparing for the distribution of your assets after death.

Core Principles of a Healthy Financial Mindset

Achieving financial health requires more than just practical financial strategies; it also necessitates cultivating a healthy financial mindset. This mindset encompasses attitudes, beliefs, and behaviors that support long-term financial well-being. Here are the core principles of a healthy financial mindset:

1. **Mindfulness and Intentionality**: Be aware of your financial habits and make intentional decisions that align with your values and goals.

This involves being conscious of your spending, saving, and investing behaviors and understanding the impact of your financial choices.

2. **Responsibility and Accountability**: Take responsibility for your financial situation and be accountable for your financial decisions. This means owning both your successes and mistakes and learning from them to improve your financial practices.

3. **Long-term Perspective**: Focus on long-term financial goals rather than immediate gratification. This requires patience and discipline, understanding that short-term sacrifices can lead to greater long-term rewards.

4. **Adaptability and Resilience**: Be prepared to adapt to changing financial circumstances and recover from setbacks. Financial resilience involves having a plan for emergencies and being able to bounce back from financial challenges.

5. **Continuous Learning**: Stay informed about financial matters and continually seek to improve your financial knowledge. This includes keeping up with changes in the financial landscape and being open to new strategies and tools.

6. **Balanced Approach**: Strive for a balance between saving, spending, and investing. A healthy financial mindset does not involve extreme frugality or reckless spending, but a

balanced approach that ensures current enjoyment and future security.

Common Financial Pitfalls and How to Avoid Them

Despite the best intentions, many people fall into common financial pitfalls that can hinder their financial health. Recognizing these pitfalls and understanding how to avoid them is crucial for maintaining a healthy financial mindset.

1. **Living Beyond Your Means**
   - **Pitfall**: Spending more than you earn is one of the most common financial mistakes. This often leads to accumulating debt and living paycheck to paycheck.
   - **Solution**: Create a realistic budget that reflects your income and prioritize living within your means. Track your spending to identify areas where you can cut back and focus on needs over wants.
2. **Lack of Emergency Savings**
   - **Pitfall**: Not having an emergency fund can leave you vulnerable to financial crises, such as unexpected medical bills or job loss.
   - **Solution**: Aim to build an emergency fund that covers three to six months of

living expenses. Start by setting aside a small amount each month and gradually increase your savings.

3. **Ignoring Debt**
   - **Pitfall**: Avoiding debt or only making minimum payments can lead to a debt spiral, especially with high-interest debt like credit cards.
   - **Solution**: Develop a debt repayment plan that prioritizes high-interest debt first. Consider using strategies like the debt snowball (paying off smallest debts first) or debt avalanche (paying off highest interest debts first).

4. **Impulse Spending**
   - **Pitfall**: Making unplanned purchases can derail your budget and long-term financial goals.
   - **Solution**: Practice mindful spending by waiting 24 hours before making non-essential purchases. This cooling-off period can help you decide if the purchase is truly necessary.

5. **Failure to Plan for the Future**
   - **Pitfall**: Not saving for retirement or other long-term goals can leave you unprepared for the future.
   - **Solution**: Start saving for retirement as early as possible, taking advantage of employer-sponsored retirement plans and tax-advantaged accounts like IRAs. Set specific, achievable long-term

financial goals and create a plan to reach them.

6. **Lack of Financial Education**
   - **Pitfall**: Not understanding basic financial concepts can lead to poor financial decisions.
   - **Solution**: Invest time in improving your financial literacy through books, courses, and reputable online resources. Seek advice from financial professionals if needed.

7. **Neglecting to Insure Against Risks**
   - **Pitfall**: Failing to have adequate insurance can result in significant financial loss in the event of an emergency.
   - **Solution**: Ensure you have sufficient insurance coverage for health, life, disability, home, and auto. Regularly review and update your insurance policies to match your current needs.

8. **Not Diversifying Investments**
   - **Pitfall**: Putting all your investments in one asset class or a few stocks can expose you to significant risk.
   - **Solution**: Diversify your investment portfolio across various asset classes, such as stocks, bonds, and real estate. This spreads risk and can lead to more stable returns over time.

9. **Ignoring Inflation and Taxes**

- o **Pitfall**: Failing to account for inflation and taxes can erode your purchasing power and investment returns.
- o **Solution**: Factor in inflation when setting long-term financial goals and consider tax-efficient investment strategies. Use tax-advantaged accounts and stay informed about changes in tax laws.

10. **Emotional Decision Making**
    - o **Pitfall**: Making financial decisions based on emotions, such as fear or greed, can lead to irrational choices.
    - o **Solution**: Base your financial decisions on logic and sound principles rather than emotions. Develop a long-term financial plan and stick to it, even during market fluctuations.

By understanding and avoiding these common financial pitfalls, you can build a strong foundation for financial health. Remember, achieving and maintaining financial well-being is a continuous journey that requires vigilance, education, and a commitment to making wise financial decisions.

CHAPTER TWO

SELF-ASSESSMENT AND GOAL SETTING

Conducting a Financial Self-Audit

A financial self-audit is the first step in taking control of your financial health. It involves a comprehensive review of your financial situation to understand where you stand, identify strengths and weaknesses, and lay the groundwork for informed decision-making.

Steps for Conducting a Financial Self-Audit

1. **Gather Financial Documents**
   o Collect all relevant financial documents, including bank statements, credit card statements, loan agreements, pay stubs, investment account statements, and insurance policies. Ensure you have records for at least the past six months to a year.
2. **Calculate Net Worth**
   o **Assets**: List all your assets, including cash, savings, investments, retirement accounts, real estate, and valuable personal property (e.g., vehicles, jewelry).
   o **Liabilities**: List all your liabilities, including mortgages, car loans, student

loans, credit card debt, and any other debts.

- o **Net Worth**: Subtract your total liabilities from your total assets to determine your net worth. This gives you a snapshot of your overall financial health.

3. **Analyze Income and Expenses**

- o **Income**: Calculate your total monthly income from all sources, including salary, bonuses, side hustles, and passive income.
- o **Expenses**: Track your monthly expenses, categorizing them into essential (e.g., housing, utilities, groceries) and discretionary (e.g., entertainment, dining out).
- o **Cash Flow**: Subtract your total monthly expenses from your total monthly income to determine your cash flow. Positive cash flow indicates that you are living within your means, while negative cash flow suggests you are spending more than you earn.

4. **Review Debt and Credit**

- o **Debt Analysis**: List all your debts, including balances, interest rates, and monthly payments. Assess which debts are high-interest and prioritize paying them off.
- o **Credit Report**: Obtain a copy of your credit report from major credit bureaus

and review it for accuracy. Note your credit score and identify areas for improvement, such as reducing credit card balances or disputing errors.

5. **Evaluate Savings and Investments**
   - **Emergency Fund**: Determine if you have an adequate emergency fund (typically three to six months of living expenses).
   - **Retirement Savings**: Review your retirement accounts and assess whether you are on track to meet your retirement goals.
   - **Investment Portfolio**: Analyze your investment portfolio to ensure it is diversified and aligned with your risk tolerance and financial goals.

6. **Insurance Coverage**
   - Review your insurance policies (health, life, disability, auto, home) to ensure you have adequate coverage. Identify any gaps and consider increasing coverage if necessary.

Identifying Financial Goals

Once you have a clear understanding of your current financial situation, the next step is to identify your financial goals. Setting clear, actionable goals provides direction and motivation, helping you stay focused on your path to financial well-being.

Types of Financial Goals

1. **Short-term Goals (0-1 year)**
   - o Examples: Building an emergency fund, paying off a credit card, saving for a vacation, creating a budget.
   - o Characteristics: These goals are specific, achievable, and have a short timeframe. They help you address immediate financial needs and build momentum.
2. **Medium-term Goals (1-5 years)**
   - o Examples: Saving for a down payment on a house, paying off student loans, buying a car, building a robust investment portfolio.
   - o Characteristics: These goals require more planning and discipline. They bridge the gap between short-term achievements and long-term aspirations.
3. **Long-term Goals (5+ years)**
   - o Examples: Saving for retirement, funding children's education, achieving financial independence, buying a vacation home.
   - o Characteristics: These goals are typically more ambitious and require sustained effort and strategic planning. They focus on your long-term financial security and lifestyle.

SMART Goals Framework

To ensure your financial goals are clear and actionable, use the SMART framework:

- **Specific**: Clearly define your goal. What exactly do you want to achieve?
- **Measurable**: Establish criteria for measuring progress. How will you track your progress and know when you've achieved your goal?
- **Achievable**: Set realistic goals that are attainable given your resources and constraints.
- **Relevant**: Ensure your goals align with your overall financial priorities and values.
- **Time-bound**: Set a specific deadline for achieving your goal.

Creating a Roadmap to Financial Success

With your financial self-audit complete and your goals identified, it's time to create a roadmap that outlines the steps needed to achieve your financial objectives. A well-structured plan will help you stay organized, focused, and motivated.

Steps to Create Your Financial Roadmap

1. **Prioritize Your Goals**
   - Rank your financial goals based on their importance and urgency. Focus on

achieving short-term goals first, as they can provide quick wins and build confidence.

2. **Break Down Goals into Actionable Steps**
   o For each goal, outline the specific steps needed to achieve it. For example, if your goal is to build an emergency fund, your steps might include setting up a dedicated savings account, automating monthly contributions, and reducing discretionary spending.

3. **Create a Budget**
   o Develop a budget that aligns with your financial goals. Ensure your budget reflects your income, essential expenses, discretionary spending, and savings/investments. Regularly review and adjust your budget to stay on track.

4. **Establish Timelines**
   o Assign deadlines to each step in your plan. Having a timeline creates a sense of urgency and helps you stay accountable. Be realistic about the time required to achieve each step.

5. **Monitor Progress**
   o Regularly review your progress toward your goals. Track your income, expenses, debt repayment, and savings to ensure you are on track. Adjust your plan as needed based on changes in your financial situation or priorities.

6. **Adjust and Adapt**
   - o Life is unpredictable, and your financial situation may change over time. Be prepared to adjust your roadmap as needed. Revisit your financial self-audit and goals periodically to ensure they remain relevant and achievable.
7. **Celebrate Milestones**
   - o Recognize and celebrate your achievements along the way. Celebrating milestones keeps you motivated and reinforces positive financial behaviors.

Example Financial Roadmap

To illustrate how to create a financial roadmap, let's consider an example:

Goal: Build an emergency fund of $10,000 in one year.

1. **Prioritize Goal**
   - o This is a high-priority short-term goal.
2. **Actionable Steps**
   - o Open a dedicated savings account for the emergency fund.
   - o Determine how much you can save monthly: $10,000 ÷ 12 months = $833 per month.

- Identify areas to reduce spending and increase savings (e.g., cutting dining out expenses, canceling unused subscriptions).
- Set up automatic transfers of $833 from your checking account to your emergency fund each month.

3. **Create a Budget**
   - Adjust your budget to allocate $833 per month to the emergency fund. Ensure other essential expenses and savings goals are still covered.

4. **Establish Timelines**
   - Monthly: Transfer $833 to the emergency fund.
   - Quarterly: Review progress and adjust as necessary.

5. **Monitor Progress**
   - Track your savings balance monthly to ensure you are on target.

6. **Adjust and Adapt**
   - If unexpected expenses arise, adjust your budget to maintain progress toward your goal. Consider ways to increase income, such as freelance work or selling unused items.

7. **Celebrate Milestones**
   - Celebrate each $2,500 milestone reached (e.g., treat yourself to a small reward like a dinner out or a movie night).

By following these steps and creating a detailed roadmap, you can effectively work toward your financial goals. Remember, the key to financial success is consistent effort, adaptability, and a positive mindset.

Conclusion

Conducting a financial self-audit, identifying financial goals, and creating a roadmap to financial success are essential steps in achieving financial health. By understanding your current financial situation, setting clear and actionable goals, and developing a structured plan, you can take control of your finances and work towards a secure and fulfilling financial future. Stay committed to your financial journey, continually reassess and adjust your plan, and celebrate your progress along the way. With dedication and discipline, you can build a healthy financial mindset and achieve lasting financial well-being.

CHAPTER THREE

MINDFULNESS AND MONEY

The Role of Mindfulness in Financial Decision Making

Mindfulness, often associated with mental and emotional well-being, plays a crucial role in financial decision-making. It involves being fully present and aware of your thoughts, feelings, and actions in the moment, without judgment. Applying mindfulness to your finances means making intentional, informed decisions that align with your values and long-term goals.

Benefits of Mindfulness in Financial Decisions

1. **Enhanced Awareness**: Mindfulness helps you become more aware of your financial habits and behaviors. By paying attention to how you earn, spend, save, and invest, you can identify patterns that support or hinder your financial well-being.
2. **Reduced Impulse Spending**: Practicing mindfulness can curb impulsive financial decisions. By taking a moment to reflect before making a purchase, you can assess whether it aligns with your values and goals, reducing the likelihood of regrettable impulse buys.

3. **Improved Emotional Regulation**: Financial decisions are often influenced by emotions such as fear, greed, or stress. Mindfulness helps you recognize these emotions and manage them effectively, leading to more rational and thoughtful financial choices.

4. **Greater Alignment with Values**: Mindfulness encourages you to consider whether your financial actions are in harmony with your personal values and long-term objectives. This alignment promotes a sense of fulfillment and purpose in your financial journey.

5. **Long-term Perspective**: Mindful financial decision-making fosters a long-term outlook. Instead of focusing on immediate gratification, you consider the future implications of your financial choices, which supports sustainable financial health.

Techniques for Practicing Financial Mindfulness

Incorporating mindfulness into your financial life requires practice and commitment. Here are several techniques to help you develop financial mindfulness:

1. **Mindful Budgeting**
   o Create a budget that reflects your income, expenses, and financial goals.

Regularly review your budget to ensure it aligns with your priorities. Use budgeting as an opportunity to practice mindfulness by tracking your spending and adjusting as needed.

2. **Reflective Spending**
   o Before making any purchase, ask yourself a series of questions: Do I need this? How does this purchase align with my values and goals? Can I afford it without compromising my financial health? This reflection helps you make intentional spending decisions.

3. **Gratitude Journaling**
   o Maintain a gratitude journal where you regularly note what you appreciate in your life, including non-material aspects. This practice shifts your focus from material possessions to meaningful experiences and relationships, reducing the urge for unnecessary spending.

4. **Mindful Saving**
   o Set clear savings goals and establish a savings plan. Each time you save, take a moment to reflect on how this action contributes to your long-term financial security and well-being. Celebrate your progress to reinforce positive saving behaviors.

5. **Regular Financial Check-ins**
   o Schedule regular financial check-ins with yourself or a financial partner.

During these sessions, review your financial situation, assess your progress toward goals, and make adjustments as needed. Use these check-ins as an opportunity to practice mindfulness and stay connected to your financial intentions.

6. **Meditation and Stress Management**
   o Incorporate meditation or other stress management techniques into your daily routine. Reducing stress improves your overall well-being and helps you approach financial decisions with a clear and calm mind.

Case Studies of Mindful Financial Choices

To illustrate the impact of mindfulness on financial decision-making, let's explore a few case studies of individuals who have successfully applied mindfulness to their financial lives.

Case Study 1: Sarah's Journey to Debt Freedom

Background: Sarah, a 30-year-old graphic designer, struggled with credit card debt for years. Her impulsive spending and lack of financial awareness led to a cycle of debt and stress.

Mindful Approach:

- **Self-Awareness**: Sarah began practicing mindfulness by tracking her spending and identifying triggers for her impulsive purchases. She realized that stress and social pressure often drove her to shop online.
- **Reflective Spending**: Before making any purchase, Sarah started asking herself if the item was a need or a want and how it would impact her debt repayment plan. This reflection helped her reduce unnecessary spending.
- **Gratitude Practice**: Sarah kept a gratitude journal, focusing on non-material sources of happiness. This practice shifted her mindset from seeking joy through purchases to finding contentment in experiences and relationships.
- **Regular Check-ins**: She scheduled weekly financial check-ins to review her budget, track her debt repayment progress, and make any necessary adjustments.

Outcome: Within two years, Sarah paid off her credit card debt. She developed healthier financial habits and experienced less stress and greater financial freedom. Her mindful approach to spending and saving became a cornerstone of her financial well-being.

Case Study 2: John's Mindful Investment Strategy

Background: John, a 45-year-old engineer, had a stable income but lacked a clear investment strategy. His investments were sporadic and often influenced by market hype and fear.

Mindful Approach:

- **Self-Awareness**: John started by assessing his risk tolerance and financial goals. He realized that his fear of market volatility often led him to make reactive investment decisions.
- **Reflective Investing**: Before making any investment, John reflected on whether it aligned with his long-term goals and risk tolerance. He avoided making decisions based on short-term market movements or emotional reactions.
- **Continuous Learning**: John committed to improving his financial literacy by reading books and attending seminars on investing. This ongoing education helped him make informed and confident investment choices.
- **Meditation Practice**: To manage stress and improve focus, John incorporated daily meditation into his routine. This practice helped him approach his investments with a calm and clear mind.

Outcome: Over five years, John built a diversified investment portfolio that aligned with his risk tolerance and long-term goals. His mindful investment strategy led to more stable and consistent returns, reducing the stress associated with market fluctuations.

Case Study 3: Lisa and Mark's Mindful Retirement Planning

Background: Lisa and Mark, a couple in their early 50s, realized they were behind on their retirement savings. Their lack of planning and awareness had left them feeling anxious about their financial future.

Mindful Approach:

- **Self-Awareness**: Lisa and Mark began by conducting a comprehensive financial self-audit to understand their current situation and retirement needs. They identified their savings gap and areas where they could cut expenses.
- **Goal Setting**: They set clear and specific retirement goals, including their desired retirement age, lifestyle, and savings targets. They used the SMART framework to make these goals actionable and achievable.
- **Regular Check-ins**: The couple scheduled monthly financial check-ins to review their

progress, adjust their budget, and ensure they were on track to meet their retirement goals.

- **Mindful Budgeting**: Lisa and Mark created a budget that prioritized their retirement savings. They made conscious decisions to reduce discretionary spending and increase their retirement contributions.
- **Stress Management**: To manage the stress of their financial catch-up plan, they practiced yoga and mindfulness meditation together. These activities helped them stay focused and motivated.

Outcome: Over the next ten years, Lisa and Mark significantly increased their retirement savings. Their mindful approach to budgeting and saving helped them feel more secure and confident about their financial future. They achieved their retirement goals and were able to retire comfortably.

Conclusion

Mindfulness can transform your financial life by enhancing your awareness, reducing impulsive behaviors, and aligning your financial decisions with your values and long-term goals. By practicing techniques such as mindful budgeting, reflective spending, gratitude journaling, and regular financial check-ins, you can cultivate a healthier relationship with money and make more intentional financial choices. The case studies of Sarah, John, and Lisa and Mark illustrate the profound impact mindfulness can have on financial well-being. Embrace mindfulness as a tool to support your financial journey and achieve lasting financial success.

CHAPTER FOUR

BUILDING POSITIVE FINANCIAL HABITS

The Psychology of Habit Formation

Habits play a significant role in shaping our daily lives, including our financial behaviors. Understanding the psychology of habit formation can help us develop positive financial habits that contribute to long-term financial well-being.

Habit Loop

According to the habit loop model proposed by Charles Duhigg in his book "The Power of Habit," habits consist of three components:

1. **Cue**: A trigger that prompts a behavior. Cues can be internal (e.g., emotions, thoughts) or external (e.g., time of day, location).
2. **Routine**: The behavior itself, which is the habitual response to the cue.
3. **Reward**: The positive reinforcement that reinforces the behavior and increases the likelihood of repetition.

How Habits Are Formed

Habits are formed through a process called "chunking," where behaviors become automatic through repetition and reinforcement. Initially, conscious effort and motivation are required to perform a behavior. Over time, as the behavior becomes habitual, less effort and conscious thought are needed.

Strategies for Habit Formation

To develop positive financial habits, consider the following strategies:

1. **Start Small**: Begin with small, achievable habits that are easy to incorporate into your daily routine. Gradually increase the complexity or difficulty of the habits over time.
2. **Consistency**: Consistently perform the desired behavior in response to the cue. Repetition is key to habit formation.
3. **Anchor Habits**: Anchor new financial habits to existing routines or cues. For example, if you want to review your budget daily, do it right after your morning coffee or before bedtime.
4. **Visual Cues**: Use visual reminders, such as sticky notes or smartphone reminders, to prompt the desired behavior.

5. **Immediate Rewards**: Associate immediate rewards with the behavior to reinforce the habit. This could be a sense of accomplishment, a small treat, or a positive affirmation.
6. **Environment Design**: Create an environment that supports the desired behavior and minimizes barriers. For example, set up automatic transfers for savings or keep healthy snacks readily available to reduce impulse spending.

Developing Daily, Weekly, and Monthly Financial Habits

Positive financial habits can be categorized into daily, weekly, and monthly routines. Incorporating these habits into your life can help you stay organized, disciplined, and focused on your financial goals.

Daily Financial Habits

1. **Track Expenses**: Review your daily expenses and categorize them to gain insight into your spending patterns.
2. **Check Account Balances**: Monitor your bank account and credit card balances daily to stay aware of your financial status.
3. **Review Budget**: Spend a few minutes each day reviewing your budget and adjusting as needed to stay on track.

4. **Practice Gratitude**: Take a moment to express gratitude for your financial blessings and successes, fostering a positive mindset towards money.

Weekly Financial Habits

1. **Plan Meals and Groceries**: Create a meal plan and grocery list for the week to minimize food waste and unnecessary spending.
2. **Review Goals**: Reflect on your financial goals and progress towards achieving them. Make any necessary adjustments to your plan.
3. **Pay Bills**: Set aside time each week to pay bills and review upcoming expenses to avoid late payments and fees.
4. **Review Savings**: Check your progress towards savings goals and adjust contributions as necessary.

Monthly Financial Habits

1. **Review Credit Report**: Obtain and review your credit report to ensure accuracy and identify any potential issues.
2. **Review Investments**: Review your investment portfolio and rebalance if necessary to maintain desired asset allocation.

3. **Evaluate Subscriptions**: Review recurring subscriptions and cancel any that are no longer necessary or unused.
4. **Set Aside Savings**: Transfer funds to your savings or investment accounts to ensure progress towards your financial goals.

Tools and Apps to Support Financial Habit Building

Technology can be a valuable tool in building and maintaining positive financial habits. There are numerous apps and tools available to help you track expenses, budget effectively, save money, and invest wisely.

Expense Tracking Apps

1. **Mint**: A popular budgeting app that automatically categorizes expenses and tracks spending across accounts.
2. **YNAB (You Need A Budget)**: A budgeting app based on the principle of giving every dollar a job, helping users prioritize spending and save money.
3. **PocketGuard**: An app that tracks spending, analyzes patterns, and suggests ways to save money.

Budgeting Apps

1. **Goodbudget**: A digital envelope system that helps users allocate funds to different spending categories and track expenses.
2. **EveryDollar**: A zero-based budgeting app that allows users to assign every dollar of income to a specific budget category.
3. **Personal Capital**: A comprehensive financial planning tool that tracks expenses, analyzes investments, and provides personalized financial advice.

Savings and Investment Apps

1. **Acorns**: An app that rounds up your purchases to the nearest dollar and invests the spare change into a diversified portfolio.
2. **Betterment**: An automated investing platform that creates and manages personalized investment portfolios based on user goals and risk tolerance.
3. **Robinhood**: A commission-free trading app that allows users to invest in stocks, ETFs, and cryptocurrencies.

Habit Tracking Apps

1. **Habitica**: A gamified habit tracking app that turns your habits into a role-playing game, rewarding you for completing tasks.

2. **Streaks**: A habit tracking app that focuses on building streaks of consecutive days for completing tasks, providing motivation to stay consistent.
3. **Coach.me**: A habit tracking app that offers coaching and accountability features to help users stay on track with their goals.

Conclusion

Building positive financial habits is essential for achieving long-term financial success. By understanding the psychology of habit formation, developing daily, weekly, and monthly financial routines, and leveraging tools and apps to support your efforts, you can cultivate habits that contribute to financial stability, security, and freedom. Stay consistent, patient, and adaptable as you work towards building and maintaining positive financial habits. With dedication and perseverance, you can transform your financial habits and achieve your financial goals.

CHAPTER FIVE

BUDGETING WITH PURPOSE

Creating a Budget that Reflects Your Values

Budgeting is not just about tracking expenses; it's about aligning your spending with your values and priorities. By creating a budget that reflects your values, you can ensure that your financial decisions are in line with what matters most to you.

Identify Your Values

1. **Reflect on What Matters**: Take time to think about your values and priorities in life. Consider what brings you joy, fulfillment, and satisfaction.
2. **Prioritize Your Values**: Rank your values in order of importance. What are the non-negotiables in your life? What are the areas where you are willing to make sacrifices?
3. **Align Spending with Values**: Review your current spending habits and assess whether they align with your values. Identify areas where your spending may be misaligned and consider adjustments.

Allocate Funds Accordingly

1. **Needs vs. Wants**: Distinguish between essential expenses (needs) and discretionary spending (wants). Allocate funds to cover your needs first before allocating money to wants.
2. **Value-Based Categories**: Create budget categories that reflect your values. For example, if family is a top priority, allocate funds for activities or experiences that strengthen family bonds.
3. **Savings and Investments**: Prioritize savings and investments that support your long-term financial goals and values, such as retirement, education, or philanthropy.

Track Your Progress

1. **Regular Review**: Periodically review your budget to ensure that your spending aligns with your values and goals. Make adjustments as needed to stay on track.
2. **Celebrate Successes**: Acknowledge and celebrate milestones along the way. Celebrating achievements reinforces positive financial behaviors and motivates you to continue.

Strategies for Sticking to Your Budget

Sticking to a budget can be challenging, but with the right strategies, it's possible to stay disciplined and accountable to your financial plan.

Set Realistic Goals

1. **Start Small**: Set achievable goals that are realistic given your income, expenses, and financial situation.
2. **Break it Down**: Break larger goals into smaller, manageable steps. Celebrate each small success along the way to maintain motivation.

Track Your Spending

1. **Use Budgeting Tools**: Utilize budgeting apps or spreadsheets to track your expenses and monitor your progress.
2. **Review Regularly**: Set aside time each week or month to review your spending and compare it to your budget. Identify any areas where you may be overspending and make adjustments as needed.

Practice Mindful Spending

1. **Reflect Before Purchasing**: Before making a purchase, ask yourself if it aligns with your values and priorities. Consider whether the item is a need or a want and if it fits within your budget.
2. **Delay Gratification**: Implement a waiting period for non-essential purchases. Give yourself time to consider whether the purchase is necessary and if it's worth the cost.

Use Cash Envelopes

1. **Allocate Cash for Categories**: Divide your budgeted amounts into cash envelopes for different spending categories (e.g., groceries, entertainment). Once the cash in each envelope is gone, refrain from spending more in that category until the next budgeting period.
2. **Visualize Spending**: Seeing the physical cash diminish as you spend helps you become more mindful of your purchases and encourages sticking to your budget.

Adjusting Your Budget as Life Changes

Life is dynamic, and your financial situation will inevitably change over time. It's essential to regularly review and adjust your budget to accommodate these changes and ensure that it remains effective.

Major Life Events

1. **Marriage or Partnership**: Combining finances with a partner may require adjustments to your budget to accommodate shared expenses and financial goals.
2. **Career Changes**: Changes in income, such as a raise, promotion, or job loss, may necessitate adjustments to your budget to reflect your new financial reality.
3. **Family Additions**: Having children or caring for aging parents may impact your expenses

and priorities, requiring modifications to your budget.

4. **Housing Changes**: Moving to a new home, whether renting or buying, can affect your housing costs and utilities, requiring budget adjustments.

Economic Conditions

1. **Inflation**: Rising prices may increase the cost of living, necessitating adjustments to your budget to account for higher expenses.
2. **Interest Rates**: Changes in interest rates can affect mortgage payments, loan rates, and savings returns, requiring adjustments to your budget.
3. **Market Fluctuations**: Economic downturns or fluctuations in the stock market may impact investment returns and income, necessitating changes to your budget and financial plan.

Lifestyle Changes

1. **New Hobbies or Interests**: Pursuing new hobbies or interests may require reallocating funds within your budget to accommodate related expenses.
2. **Health and Wellness**: Investing in health and wellness activities, such as gym memberships or healthy eating habits, may require adjustments to your budget to prioritize these expenses.

3. **Travel and Leisure**: Changes in travel plans or leisure activities may impact your discretionary spending, requiring modifications to your budget.

How to Adjust Your Budget

1. **Assess Changes**: Regularly assess your financial situation and identify any changes that may require adjustments to your budget.
2. **Review Priorities**: Revisit your values and financial goals to ensure they align with your current circumstances and priorities.
3. **Reallocation**: Reallocate funds within your budget to accommodate changes in expenses or income. Consider reducing spending in non-essential categories to free up funds for new priorities.
4. **Communicate and Collaborate**: If applicable, discuss budget adjustments with your partner or family members to ensure everyone is on the same page and committed to the new financial plan.

Conclusion

Budgeting with purpose involves aligning your spending with your values, developing strategies to stick to your budget, and adjusting as life changes. By creating a budget that reflects your values, tracking your spending, and practicing mindful spending, you can stay disciplined and accountable to your financial plan. Regularly review and adjust your budget to accommodate life changes and ensure that it remains effective in helping you achieve your financial goals. With purposeful budgeting, you can take control of your finances and build a secure and fulfilling future.

CHAPTER SIX

SMART SAVING AND INVESTING

Understanding Saving vs. Investing

Saving and investing are two essential components of financial planning, each serving distinct purposes in helping individuals achieve their financial goals.

Saving

1. **Purpose**: Saving involves setting aside money for short-term goals and emergencies, typically in low-risk, easily accessible accounts such as savings accounts or certificates of deposit (CDs).
2. **Goal**: The primary goal of saving is to build a financial safety net, cover unexpected expenses, and achieve short-term objectives such as buying a car, taking a vacation, or making a down payment on a home.
3. **Characteristics**: Savings are generally low risk and liquid, meaning they can be easily accessed in case of emergencies or short-term needs.

Investing

1. **Purpose**: Investing involves putting money into assets with the expectation of generating

returns over the long term, typically in higher-risk vehicles such as stocks, bonds, mutual funds, or real estate.

2. **Goal**: The primary goal of investing is to grow wealth and achieve long-term financial objectives, such as retirement savings, funding education, or building wealth for future generations.

3. **Characteristics**: Investments carry varying degrees of risk and may experience fluctuations in value over time. However, they have the potential for higher returns compared to savings accounts.

Building an Emergency Fund

An emergency fund is a crucial component of financial planning, providing a financial safety net to cover unexpected expenses and financial setbacks.

Importance of an Emergency Fund

1. **Financial Security**: An emergency fund provides peace of mind and financial security, allowing individuals to handle unexpected expenses without resorting to high-interest debt or depleting savings meant for other goals.

2. **Stability**: Having an emergency fund helps individuals navigate unforeseen events such as job loss, medical emergencies, car repairs, or

home repairs without disrupting their financial stability.

3. **Avoiding Debt**: An adequately funded emergency fund reduces the need to rely on credit cards or loans to cover unexpected expenses, minimizing interest costs and avoiding the accumulation of debt.

How to Build an Emergency Fund

1. **Set a Goal**: Determine how much you need to save for emergencies, typically three to six months' worth of living expenses. Adjust the target based on your individual circumstances, such as job stability, dependents, and financial obligations.

2. **Automate Savings**: Set up automatic transfers from your checking account to a dedicated emergency savings account each month. Treat the emergency fund as a non-negotiable expense to ensure consistent contributions.

3. **Prioritize**: Make building your emergency fund a priority in your budgeting and financial planning. Cut discretionary spending or find additional sources of income to accelerate savings growth.

4. **Keep it Separate**: Maintain your emergency fund in a separate, easily accessible account, such as a high-yield savings account or a

money market account. Avoid investing emergency funds in assets that may experience volatility or have withdrawal restrictions.

Introduction to Investment Strategies

Investing is a powerful tool for growing wealth over the long term, but it requires careful planning, research, and risk management.

Investment Goals and Time Horizon

1. **Define Objectives**: Clarify your investment goals, such as retirement savings, wealth accumulation, or funding major expenses like education or a home purchase.
2. **Consider Time Horizon**: Determine your investment time horizon, or the length of time you expect to hold your investments. Longer time horizons generally allow for more aggressive investment strategies, while shorter time horizons may require more conservative approaches.

Asset Allocation

1. **Diversification**: Spread your investments across different asset classes, such as stocks, bonds, real estate, and cash equivalents, to reduce risk and optimize returns.

2. **Risk Tolerance**: Assess your risk tolerance, or your ability and willingness to endure fluctuations in the value of your investments. Choose an asset allocation that aligns with your risk tolerance and investment goals.

3. **Rebalance Regularly**: Periodically review and rebalance your investment portfolio to maintain your desired asset allocation. Rebalancing ensures that your portfolio remains aligned with your risk tolerance and investment objectives.

Investment Vehicles

1. **Stocks**: Stocks represent ownership in a company and offer the potential for capital appreciation and dividends. They tend to be more volatile but offer higher long-term returns.

2. **Bonds**: Bonds are debt securities issued by governments, municipalities, or corporations. They provide regular interest payments and return the principal amount at maturity. Bonds are generally less volatile than stocks but offer lower returns.

3. **Mutual Funds and ETFs**: Mutual funds and exchange-traded funds (ETFs) pool investors' money to invest in a diversified portfolio of stocks, bonds, or other assets. They offer

diversification and professional management but may charge fees.

4. **Real Estate**: Real estate investments involve purchasing property or investing in real estate investment trusts (REITs) to generate rental income and capital appreciation. Real estate can provide diversification and income but requires careful management and may be illiquid.

5. **Retirement Accounts**: Retirement accounts such as 401(k)s, IRAs, and Roth IRAs offer tax advantages for long-term savings. Take advantage of employer-sponsored retirement plans and contribute regularly to maximize tax benefits and retirement savings.

Risk Management

1. **Asset Allocation**: Diversify your investments across different asset classes to reduce risk and volatility. A well-diversified portfolio can help mitigate the impact of market fluctuations on your overall investment returns.

2. **Emergency Fund**: Maintain an adequate emergency fund to cover unexpected expenses and financial setbacks. Having a financial safety net allows you to withstand short-term market downturns without needing to sell investments at a loss.

3. **Regular Review**: Periodically review your investment portfolio and performance to ensure it remains aligned with your goals and risk tolerance. Consider adjustments as needed based on changes in your financial situation or market conditions.

Conclusion

Smart saving and investing are essential components of financial planning, helping individuals achieve short-term objectives and long-term financial goals. By understanding the differences between saving and investing, building an emergency fund, and developing investment strategies that align with your goals and risk tolerance, you can build wealth and secure your financial future. Start with a solid foundation of saving and emergency planning before venturing into investment opportunities, and regularly review and adjust your financial plan to stay on track towards achieving your financial objectives. With careful planning and disciplined execution, you can optimize your financial resources and build a prosperous future.

CHAPTER SEVEN

MANAGING DEBT WISELY

Types of Debt and Their Impacts

Debt can be a double-edged sword, providing access to necessary resources and opportunities while also posing risks to financial stability and well-being. Understanding the different types of debt and their impacts is crucial for effective debt management.

Types of Debt

1. **Good Debt**:
   - **Mortgages**: Loans used to purchase a home or real estate. Mortgage debt is considered good debt as it allows individuals to build equity and potentially benefit from property appreciation.
   - **Student Loans**: Loans used to finance education and skill development. While student loans can be substantial, they are considered an investment in future earning potential.
   - **Business Loans**: Loans used to start or expand a business. Business debt can be considered good if it leads to

increased profitability and growth opportunities.

2. **Bad Debt**:

   - **Credit Card Debt**: High-interest debt accumulated through credit card purchases. Credit card debt can quickly spiral out of control if not managed responsibly.
   - **Payday Loans**: Short-term, high-cost loans typically used to cover emergency expenses. Payday loans often come with exorbitant interest rates and fees, trapping borrowers in a cycle of debt.
   - **Auto Loans**: Loans used to purchase vehicles. While auto loans can be necessary for transportation, excessive debt or high-interest rates can strain finances.

Impacts of Debt

1. **Financial Strain**: Excessive debt can lead to financial stress, making it challenging to cover living expenses, save for the future, or achieve financial goals.
2. **High Interest Costs**: Accumulating interest on debt can significantly increase the total amount repaid over time, reducing available funds for other priorities.
3. **Credit Score**: Debt levels and repayment history impact credit scores, affecting access to

credit, loan terms, and interest rates for future borrowing.

4. **Limited Opportunities**: High levels of debt may limit opportunities for homeownership, entrepreneurship, and overall financial freedom.

Strategies for Debt Reduction and Management

Managing debt wisely involves developing a strategic plan to reduce debt levels, minimize interest costs, and regain financial control.

Debt Repayment Strategies

1. **Debt Snowball Method**: Prioritize paying off debts from smallest to largest balance regardless of interest rate. As each debt is paid off, apply the freed-up payment to the next debt.

2. **Debt Avalanche Method**: Focus on paying off debts with the highest interest rates first while making minimum payments on other debts. Once the highest-interest debt is paid off, allocate the payment to the next highest-interest debt.

3. **Debt Consolidation**: Combine multiple debts into a single loan with a lower interest rate, streamlining payments and potentially reducing overall interest costs.

4. **Balance Transfer**: Transfer high-interest credit card balances to a card with a lower promotional interest rate, allowing more payments to go towards principal repayment.

Budgeting and Expense Management

1. **Create a Budget**: Develop a realistic budget that allocates funds towards debt repayment while covering essential expenses and savings goals.
2. **Cut Discretionary Spending**: Identify areas where spending can be reduced or eliminated to free up funds for debt repayment. Consider cutting unnecessary subscriptions, dining out less frequently, or finding cheaper alternatives for entertainment.
3. **Increase Income**: Explore opportunities to increase income through side gigs, freelance work, or asking for a raise at work. Additional income can accelerate debt repayment and improve financial stability.

Negotiate with Creditors

1. **Interest Rate Reduction**: Contact creditors to negotiate lower interest rates, especially on high-interest credit card debt. A lower interest

rate can significantly reduce the total cost of debt over time.

2. **Payment Plans**: Request a more manageable repayment plan, such as extended terms or reduced monthly payments, to make debt repayment more affordable.

Maintaining a Debt-Free Lifestyle

Achieving debt freedom is a significant accomplishment, but maintaining a debt-free lifestyle requires ongoing discipline and commitment.

Build Emergency Savings

1. **Establish an Emergency Fund**: Build a robust emergency fund to cover unexpected expenses and financial setbacks without resorting to debt.

Live Within Your Means

1. **Avoid Lifestyle Inflation**: Resist the temptation to increase spending as income rises. Instead, prioritize saving and investing to build long-term wealth.
2. **Pay Cash for Purchases**: Whenever possible, pay cash for purchases rather than relying on credit cards or loans. This practice encourages mindful spending and avoids accumulating new debt.

Continuously Review and Adjust

1. **Regular Financial Check-ins**: Schedule regular reviews of your finances to assess progress towards financial goals, identify areas for improvement, and make necessary adjustments.

2. **Stay Committed to Financial Goals**: Maintain focus on long-term financial goals and priorities, such as retirement savings, homeownership, or education funding. Avoid taking on unnecessary debt that detracts from these goals.

Conclusion

Managing debt wisely is essential for achieving financial stability and building long-term wealth. By understanding the different types of debt, implementing effective debt repayment strategies, and maintaining a debt-free lifestyle, individuals can regain control of their finances and achieve financial freedom. Prioritize debt repayment, develop a realistic budget, and make strategic financial decisions to reduce debt levels and minimize interest costs. With diligence, discipline, and perseverance, anyone can achieve debt freedom and secure a brighter financial future.

CHAPTER EIGHT

FINANCIAL EDUCATION AND CONTINUOUS LEARNING

The Importance of Financial Literacy

Financial literacy is the foundation of sound financial decision-making and empowerment. It equips individuals with the knowledge, skills, and confidence to manage their finances effectively, navigate complex financial products and services, and achieve their financial goals.

Empowerment and Independence

1. **Informed Decision Making**: Financial literacy enables individuals to make informed decisions about saving, investing, borrowing, and spending, aligning their actions with their long-term goals and values.
2. **Risk Management**: Understanding financial concepts such as risk, diversification, and asset allocation helps individuals manage financial risks and build resilience against unforeseen events.

Breaking the Cycle of Debt and Poverty

1. **Debt Avoidance**: Financial literacy empowers individuals to avoid high-cost debt traps, make responsible borrowing decisions, and prioritize debt repayment strategies.
2. **Wealth Building**: By understanding the principles of saving, investing, and wealth accumulation, individuals can break the cycle of poverty and build generational wealth for themselves and their families.

Access to Opportunities

1. **Entrepreneurship**: Financial literacy fosters entrepreneurial spirit by equipping individuals with the knowledge and skills to start and manage successful businesses, driving economic growth and innovation.
2. **Homeownership**: Understanding mortgage products, down payment requirements, and homeownership costs enables individuals to make informed decisions about purchasing and maintaining homes, promoting housing stability and wealth accumulation.

Resources for Ongoing Financial Education

Continuous learning is essential for staying informed about evolving financial trends, products, and strategies. Fortunately, there are numerous resources available to support ongoing financial education and skill development.

Books and Publications

1. **Personal Finance Books**: Explore a variety of personal finance books covering topics such as budgeting, investing, retirement planning, and debt management.
2. **Financial Magazines**: Subscribe to financial magazines and publications for insights into market trends, investment strategies, and economic analysis.

Online Courses and Webinars

1. **Financial Literacy Courses**: Enroll in online courses or webinars offered by reputable institutions, covering topics ranging from basic budgeting to advanced investment strategies.
2. **Investment Platforms**: Many investment platforms offer educational resources, tutorials, and webinars to help users understand investment products and strategies.

Financial Blogs and Podcasts

1. **Personal Finance Blogs**: Follow personal finance bloggers who share practical tips, strategies, and insights on managing money, investing, and achieving financial goals.
2. **Financial Podcasts**: Listen to financial podcasts featuring interviews with experts, discussions on financial topics, and real-life stories of financial success and challenges.

Staying Informed in a Changing Financial Landscape

The financial landscape is constantly evolving, driven by technological advancements, regulatory changes, and economic shifts. Staying informed and adaptable is essential for navigating these changes effectively.

Regular Information Consumption

1. **News Outlets**: Stay updated on financial news, market developments, and economic indicators through reputable news outlets, websites, and financial publications.
2. **Industry Reports**: Access industry reports, research papers, and whitepapers to gain insights into emerging trends, market opportunities, and regulatory changes.

Engage with Financial Professionals

1. **Financial Advisors**: Consult with certified financial advisors or planners to receive personalized financial guidance, investment recommendations, and retirement planning strategies.
2. **Accountants and Tax Professionals**: Work with accountants and tax professionals to optimize tax efficiency, minimize tax liabilities, and ensure compliance with tax regulations.

Networking and Community Engagement

1. **Financial Workshops and Seminars**: Attend financial workshops, seminars, and networking events to connect with industry professionals, share knowledge, and learn from peers.
2. **Online Forums and Communities**: Join online forums, social media groups, and community platforms focused on personal finance and investing to engage in discussions, ask questions, and share insights.

Conclusion

Financial education and continuous learning are essential for building financial literacy, empowerment, and resilience. By investing in ongoing education and skill development, individuals can make informed financial decisions, avoid common pitfalls, and achieve their financial goals. Explore a variety of resources, including books, online courses, webinars, blogs, podcasts, and industry reports, to stay informed about personal finance, investing, and economic trends. Stay proactive, adaptable, and engaged with financial professionals and communities to navigate the ever-changing financial landscape with confidence and competence. With a commitment to lifelong learning, anyone can build a solid foundation for financial success and prosperity.

CHAPTER NINE

NAVIGATING FINANCIAL CHALLENGES

Preparing for Financial Setbacks

Financial challenges are inevitable aspects of life, ranging from unexpected expenses and job loss to economic downturns and market volatility. While it's impossible to predict every financial setback, proactive planning and preparation can help individuals weather storms with greater resilience.

Building an Emergency Fund

1. **Emergency Savings**: Establish an emergency fund to cover essential expenses in the event of job loss, medical emergencies, or unforeseen expenses. Aim to save three to six months' worth of living expenses in a liquid, easily accessible account.
2. **Budgeting**: Create a realistic budget that prioritizes savings and contingency planning. Allocate funds towards emergency savings as part of your regular budgeting process.
3. **Insurance Coverage**: Review insurance policies, including health, disability, life, and

property insurance, to ensure adequate coverage in case of unexpected events.

Emotional Resilience and Financial Stress

Financial challenges often come with emotional stress and anxiety, impacting mental health and overall well-being. Developing emotional resilience and coping strategies is essential for navigating financial adversity with grace and resilience.

Mindfulness and Stress Management

1. **Mindfulness Practices**: Incorporate mindfulness meditation, deep breathing exercises, and stress-relief techniques into your daily routine to manage anxiety and promote emotional well-being.
2. **Physical Activity**: Engage in regular physical activity, such as exercise, yoga, or walking, to reduce stress levels, improve mood, and boost resilience.
3. **Seek Support**: Reach out to friends, family, or mental health professionals for support and guidance during challenging times. Sharing your concerns and feelings can provide comfort and perspective.

Real-life Stories of Overcoming Financial Adversity

Real-life stories of individuals overcoming financial adversity serve as sources of inspiration and motivation, demonstrating resilience, determination, and creativity in the face of challenges.

Case Studies and Success Stories

1. **Job Loss and Recovery**: Learn from individuals who have successfully navigated job loss, including strategies for finding new employment, managing finances during unemployment, and rebuilding career paths.
2. **Debt Repayment Journeys**: Explore stories of individuals who have conquered debt, implemented effective repayment strategies, and achieved financial freedom through discipline and perseverance.
3. **Financial Comebacks**: Discover stories of individuals who have bounced back from financial setbacks, such as bankruptcy, foreclosure, or investment losses, by learning from mistakes, seeking professional advice, and staying resilient.

Conclusion

Navigating financial challenges requires a combination of proactive planning, emotional resilience, and determination. By preparing for financial setbacks, developing coping strategies for managing stress, and drawing inspiration from real-life success stories, individuals can overcome adversity and emerge stronger and more resilient. Remember that financial challenges are temporary setbacks on the path to long-term financial well-being. Stay focused on your goals, lean on your support network for guidance and encouragement, and trust in your ability to overcome obstacles with resilience and determination. With the right mindset and strategies, you can navigate financial challenges with grace and emerge stronger on the other side.

CHAPTER TEN

CULTIVATING A GENEROUS MINDSET

The Role of Giving in Financial Health

Generosity is not only a virtue but also a fundamental aspect of financial health and overall well-being. While financial health involves managing one's finances responsibly, it also encompasses giving back to others and contributing to the welfare of society.

Psychological Benefits

1. **Sense of Purpose**: Giving to others provides a sense of purpose and fulfillment, contributing to overall happiness and life satisfaction.
2. **Gratitude and Appreciation**: Practicing generosity fosters feelings of gratitude and appreciation for one's own blessings, shifting focus from scarcity to abundance.
3. **Connection and Community**: Giving back strengthens social connections and fosters a sense of community, creating bonds with others who share similar values and goals.

Ways to Give Back and Support Others

There are countless ways to give back and support others, regardless of financial resources or personal circumstances. From monetary donations to acts of kindness and volunteerism, everyone has the power to make a positive impact in their communities and beyond.

Monetary Donations

1. **Charitable Organizations**: Support charitable organizations and nonprofits that align with your values and causes, whether it's education, healthcare, environmental conservation, or social justice.
2. **Crowdfunding Campaigns**: Contribute to crowdfunding campaigns for individuals or families facing financial hardship, medical emergencies, or other challenges.
3. **Tithing and Religious Offerings**: Allocate a portion of your income towards religious offerings, tithes, or donations to support religious institutions and charitable initiatives.

Acts of Kindness

1. **Random Acts of Kindness**: Perform random acts of kindness, such as paying for someone's meal, offering a helping hand to a neighbor, or volunteering your time to assist those in need.

2. **Volunteerism**: Dedicate your time and skills to volunteer work, whether it's mentoring youth, serving meals at a soup kitchen, or participating in community clean-up efforts.
3. **Skill Sharing**: Share your expertise and knowledge with others through teaching, coaching, or mentorship programs, empowering individuals to learn and grow.

Social Impact Investments

1. **Socially Responsible Investing**: Invest in socially responsible funds or companies that prioritize environmental, social, and governance (ESG) criteria, promoting positive social and environmental impact alongside financial returns.
2. **Microfinance**: Support microfinance initiatives that provide financial services to underserved communities and entrepreneurs in developing countries, empowering individuals to lift themselves out of poverty through entrepreneurship and economic opportunity.

Balancing Generosity and Personal Financial Goals

While cultivating a generous mindset is important, it's also essential to balance generosity with personal financial goals and responsibilities. By practicing mindful giving and aligning generosity with financial priorities, individuals can make meaningful contributions without compromising their own financial well-being.

Set Giving Goals

1. **Budget for Giving**: Incorporate charitable giving into your budget, allocating a specific percentage of your income towards charitable donations or philanthropic causes.
2. **Prioritize Causes**: Identify causes and organizations that resonate with your values and passions, focusing your giving efforts on areas where you can make the greatest impact.
3. **Track Impact**: Monitor and track the impact of your giving over time, celebrating milestones and accomplishments while staying accountable to your giving goals.

Practice Mindful Giving

1. **Give Within Means**: Give within your means and avoid overextending yourself financially. Prioritize personal financial stability and

sustainability while still making meaningful contributions.

2. **Research and Verify**: Research charitable organizations and initiatives to ensure transparency, accountability, and effectiveness in their programs and operations.

3. **Evaluate Impact**: Evaluate the impact of your giving efforts to ensure that your contributions are making a meaningful difference in the lives of others and the communities you serve.

Conclusion

Cultivating a generous mindset is an integral part of financial health and overall well-being. By embracing the role of giving in financial health, exploring various ways to give back and support others, and balancing generosity with personal financial goals, individuals can make a positive impact in their communities and the world. Remember that generosity is not limited to monetary donations; acts of kindness, volunteerism, and social impact investments also play a crucial role in creating positive change. By practicing mindful giving and aligning generosity with personal values and priorities, individuals can experience the joy and fulfillment that comes from making a difference in the lives of others.

CHAPTER ELEVEN

PLANNING FOR THE FUTURE

Long-term Financial Planning

Planning for the future involves taking proactive steps to secure financial stability, achieve long-term goals, and prepare for life's uncertainties. Long-term financial planning encompasses various aspects of personal finance, including retirement savings, investment strategies, and estate planning.

Setting Long-term Goals

1. **Financial Independence**: Define your vision of financial independence and the lifestyle you aspire to in the future. Consider factors such as retirement age, desired standard of living, and major life milestones.
2. **Wealth Accumulation**: Establish goals for wealth accumulation, such as saving for a down payment on a home, funding education expenses, or building a retirement nest egg.
3. **Legacy Planning**: Determine your legacy goals, including charitable giving, leaving an inheritance for loved ones, or supporting causes you care about.

Creating a Financial Plan

1. **Assess Financial Situation**: Evaluate your current financial situation, including income, expenses, assets, liabilities, and cash flow. Identify areas for improvement and opportunities for growth.
2. **Develop Strategies**: Develop strategies to achieve your long-term financial goals, such as budgeting, saving, investing, and debt management. Consider factors such as risk tolerance, time horizon, and tax implications.
3. **Monitor and Adjust**: Regularly monitor your progress towards your financial goals and adjust your plan as needed based on changes in your life circumstances, financial markets, and economic conditions.

Retirement Strategies and Considerations

Planning for retirement is a critical aspect of long-term financial planning, ensuring financial security and independence in your later years. Retirement strategies involve saving diligently, investing wisely, and making informed decisions about retirement accounts and income sources.

Retirement Savings Vehicles

1. **Employer-sponsored Plans**: Take advantage of employer-sponsored retirement plans, such as 401(k)s or 403(b)s, and contribute enough to maximize employer matching contributions.
2. **Individual Retirement Accounts (IRAs)**: Consider opening and contributing to traditional or Roth IRAs to supplement employer-sponsored retirement savings and benefit from tax advantages.
3. **Health Savings Accounts (HSAs)**: Contribute to HSAs if eligible, using them to save for qualified medical expenses in retirement while enjoying tax benefits.

Investment Strategies

1. **Asset Allocation**: Determine an appropriate asset allocation strategy based on your risk tolerance, time horizon, and retirement goals. Consider diversifying investments across asset classes to manage risk and optimize returns.
2. **Lifecycle Investing**: Consider a lifecycle or target-date fund that automatically adjusts asset allocation based on your expected retirement date, gradually shifting towards a more conservative investment mix as you approach retirement.

3. **Regular Rebalancing**: Periodically review and rebalance your retirement portfolio to maintain your desired asset allocation and adapt to changing market conditions.

Retirement Income Planning

1. **Social Security**: Understand how Social Security benefits work and plan strategically to maximize your benefits, such as delaying claiming benefits to increase monthly payments.
2. **Pension Benefits**: If eligible, factor pension benefits into your retirement income plan and consider options for receiving benefits, such as lump-sum payments or annuities.
3. **Withdrawal Strategies**: Develop a withdrawal strategy for tapping into retirement accounts in retirement, considering factors such as required minimum distributions (RMDs), tax implications, and sustainable withdrawal rates.

Estate Planning Basics

Estate planning involves making arrangements for the transfer of your assets and the distribution of your estate upon your death. It ensures that your wishes are carried out and that your loved ones are provided for according to your intentions.

Essential Components

1. **Wills and Trusts**: Create a will to specify how you want your assets to be distributed and designate beneficiaries for your estate. Consider setting up trusts to manage assets, provide for minor children, or minimize estate taxes.
2. **Power of Attorney**: Designate a trusted individual to make financial and healthcare decisions on your behalf in the event of incapacity.
3. **Healthcare Directives**: Prepare advance directives, such as a living will or healthcare power of attorney, to outline your preferences for medical care and end-of-life decisions.

Review and Update Regularly

1. **Life Events**: Review and update your estate plan periodically, especially after major life events such as marriage, divorce, birth of children or grandchildren, or changes in financial circumstances.
2. **Beneficiary Designations**: Ensure that beneficiary designations on retirement accounts, life insurance policies, and other

accounts are up to date and aligned with your estate plan.

3. **Legal Assistance**: Seek guidance from estate planning professionals, such as attorneys or financial advisors, to ensure that your estate plan is legally valid and comprehensive.

Conclusion

Planning for the future involves careful consideration of long-term financial goals, retirement strategies, and estate planning essentials. By setting clear goals, developing sound financial plans, and making informed decisions about retirement savings, investments, and estate planning, individuals can achieve financial security and peace of mind for themselves and their loved ones. Remember to regularly review and update your financial plans, adapt to changing circumstances, and seek professional guidance when needed. With thoughtful planning and proactive preparation, you can build a solid foundation for a secure and fulfilling future.

CHAPTER TWELVE

LIVING A FINANCIALLY FULFILLED LIFE

Aligning Money with Your Life Purpose

Living a financially fulfilled life goes beyond mere accumulation of wealth; it involves aligning your financial decisions with your life purpose, values, and aspirations. By connecting money with meaning, individuals can derive deeper satisfaction and fulfillment from their financial journey.

Clarifying Life Purpose

1. **Reflect on Values**: Identify your core values, passions, and priorities in life. Consider what truly matters to you and how you want to make a positive impact in the world.
2. **Define Life Purpose**: Determine your life purpose or mission statement, articulating your overarching goals and aspirations for your life journey.
3. **Align Financial Choices**: Align your financial choices, including spending, saving, investing, and giving, with your life purpose and values. Ensure that your financial decisions support your broader goals and contribute to your sense of fulfillment and well-being.

Achieving Financial Independence

Financial independence is a key milestone on the path to living a financially fulfilled life. It represents the freedom to make choices based on personal preferences rather than financial constraints, empowering individuals to live life on their own terms.

Building Wealth

1. **Save and Invest Wisely**: Practice disciplined saving and investing habits to build wealth over time. Maximize opportunities for growth and compounding by investing in diversified assets aligned with your risk tolerance and financial goals.
2. **Control Spending**: Adopt a mindful approach to spending, distinguishing between needs and wants, and prioritizing purchases that align with your values and long-term goals.
3. **Generate Passive Income**: Explore opportunities to generate passive income streams, such as rental properties, dividend-paying investments, or online business ventures, to supplement earned income and accelerate progress towards financial independence.

Creating Financial Security

1. **Emergency Savings**: Maintain an adequate emergency fund to cover unexpected expenses and financial setbacks, providing a financial safety net during challenging times.
2. **Debt Management**: Manage debt responsibly by prioritizing high-interest debt repayment, minimizing interest costs, and avoiding unnecessary borrowing.
3. **Insurance Coverage**: Protect against financial risks by securing appropriate insurance coverage, including health insurance, disability insurance, life insurance, and property insurance, to mitigate potential losses and liabilities.

Celebrating Financial Milestones

Celebrating financial milestones along the journey towards financial fulfillment acknowledges progress, reinforces positive behaviors, and provides motivation to continue striving towards financial goals.

Milestone Markers

1. **Debt-Free Milestone**: Celebrate paying off debt and achieving debt freedom, whether it's credit card debt, student loans, or a mortgage.

Acknowledge the hard work and discipline required to eliminate debt and embrace the newfound financial freedom.

2. **Retirement Savings Milestone**: Recognize reaching key milestones in retirement savings, such as reaching a specific savings target, maximizing contributions to retirement accounts, or achieving financial independence to retire on your own terms.

3. **Generosity Milestone**: Celebrate milestones in generosity and giving back, whether it's reaching a certain level of charitable donations, volunteering a significant amount of time, or making a meaningful impact in your community.

Rituals and Rewards

1. **Financial Review Rituals**: Establish regular rituals for reviewing financial progress, such as monthly budget meetings, quarterly check-ins, or annual financial assessments. Celebrate achievements and identify areas for improvement.

2. **Reward Yourself**: Treat yourself to rewards or experiences that align with your values and financial goals, such as a memorable vacation, a special purchase, or a meaningful charitable donation, to commemorate milestones and reinforce positive behaviors.

3. **Share Successes**: Share financial successes and milestones with loved ones, friends, or mentors, celebrating achievements together and fostering a supportive community of encouragement and accountability.

Conclusion

Living a financially fulfilled life involves aligning money with purpose, achieving financial independence, and celebrating milestones along the way. By connecting financial decisions with personal values, aspirations, and life purpose, individuals can derive greater satisfaction and fulfillment from their financial journey. Strive to achieve financial independence by building wealth, creating financial security, and generating passive income streams. Celebrate financial milestones, big and small, with rituals, rewards, and shared experiences, recognizing progress and reinforcing positive behaviors. With intentionality, discipline, and gratitude, anyone can live a financially fulfilled life and create a brighter future for themselves and their loved ones.

CONCLUSION

SUSTAINING A HEALTHY FINANCIAL MINDSET

As you conclude your journey towards building a healthy financial mindset, it's essential to reflect on your progress, adapt to life's changes, and keep the momentum going to sustain your newfound habits and behaviors. Here's how you can ensure the sustainability of your financial journey:

Reviewing Your Financial Journey

1. **Reflect on Achievements**: Take time to review and celebrate your financial achievements, whether it's paying off debt, reaching savings goals, or making progress towards financial independence. Acknowledge the hard work and dedication that has brought you this far.

2. **Assess Areas for Improvement**: Identify areas for improvement and growth in your financial journey. Consider where you can refine your budget, optimize your investments, or enhance your financial literacy to continue progressing towards your goals.

3. **Set New Goals**: Set new financial goals and aspirations based on your evolving priorities and life circumstances. Whether it's saving for a major purchase, investing in education or career development, or planning for

retirement, continue setting meaningful goals to guide your financial decisions.

Adapting to Life's Financial Changes

1. **Expect the Unexpected**: Anticipate and prepare for life's financial changes, such as job transitions, family milestones, economic fluctuations, or unexpected expenses. Build resilience by maintaining emergency savings and staying flexible in your financial plans.
2. **Seek Support**: Don't hesitate to seek support and guidance from financial professionals, mentors, or support networks during times of uncertainty or transition. Draw on their expertise and experience to navigate challenges and make informed decisions.
3. **Embrace Lifelong Learning**: Commit to lifelong learning and continuous improvement in your financial knowledge and skills. Stay informed about evolving financial trends, products, and strategies to adapt to changing circumstances and seize new opportunities.

Keeping the Momentum Going

1. **Stay Disciplined**: Maintain discipline and consistency in your financial habits and behaviors. Stick to your budget, continue saving and investing regularly, and resist the

temptation to overspend or deviate from your long-term financial goals.

2. **Celebrate Small Wins**: Celebrate small victories and milestones along the way to keep yourself motivated and engaged. Recognize progress, no matter how incremental, and use it as fuel to propel you forward in your financial journey.

3. **Stay Connected**: Stay connected with like-minded individuals who share your commitment to financial health and well-being. Surround yourself with a supportive community of friends, family, or peers who can encourage and inspire you on your journey.

In Conclusion

Building and sustaining a healthy financial mindset is not a destination but a lifelong journey. By reviewing your progress, adapting to life's changes, and keeping the momentum going, you can continue to cultivate financial health, resilience, and fulfillment. Remember that your financial journey is unique to you, and there is no one-size-fits-all approach to success. Stay committed to your goals, stay flexible in your plans, and stay mindful of the values and priorities that guide you on your path to financial well-being. With perseverance, determination, and a healthy financial mindset, you can create a brighter and more secure future for yourself and those you care about.